The

Quintessential Bathroom Companion

Best Wishes

Michael A. Lee

The
Quintessential
Bathroom
Companion

by

Michael A. Lee

Wessenden Valley Books

First published in Great Britain in 2004 by

Wessenden Valley Books
10 Woodlea Avenue
Oakes
Huddersfield HD3 4EF
West Yorkshire
www.written-in-jest.co.uk

British Library Cataloguing in Publication Data
A catalogue record for this book is available from The British Library.

ISBN 0 9548047 0 8

Produced by

Central Publishing Services
Royd Street Offices
Milnsbridge
Huddersfield
West Yorkshire
HD3 4QY

www.centralpublishing.co.uk

This book is dedicated to Thomas Crapper & Co. Ltd.

Thomas Crapper, the founder of the company, was born in Yorkshire in 1836.
After serving his apprenticeship to a Master Plumber he set up in his own right as a
plumber in Chelsea in 1861 quickly establishing a reputation for quality and service.

Thomas Crapper was the inventor of various ingenious sanitary fittings such as the 'Water-
Waste-Preventing Cistern System', the ' Disconnecting trap' and even.
a spring loaded loo seat.
It was also he who originated and championed the concept of the Bathroom Showroom.
Words derived from his name are, of course, well known worldwide.

By the 1880s Thomas Crapper & Co. Ltd had such a superb reputation in the field of
manufacturing and promoting sanitary appliances that he and his colleagues were invited
to supply The Prince of Wales [later Edward VII] at Sandringham.
Windsor Castle, Buckingham Palace and Westminster Abbey all benefited from Crapper
goods and services.
One could say that there was a mutually beneficial link – or could it be chain – between
those who built thrones and those who sat upon them!

Although Thomas Crapper himself died in 1910 the distinguished firm he established has
survived under the original name and continues to manufacture and provide the finest of
bathroom fittings and the worlds' most authentic period-style sanitary ware from the
Victorian and Edwardian periods.

The contact details of Thomas Crapper & Co. Ltd are as follows

Thomas Crapper & Co. Ltd
The Stable Yard
Alscot Park
Stratford-on-Avon
Warwickshire CV37 8BL

Tel : 01789 450522

Fax : 01789 450523

Email : wc@thomas-crapper.com

Website : www.thomas-crapper.com

Introduction

I doubt that anyone would disagree with the suggestion that much meditation and cogitation occurs within the various bathrooms and toilets of Great Britain everyday.

Indeed, it is most probable that great decisions of broad-ranging consequence are made whilst sitting on the porcelain thrones of Parliament, office, University and home alike.

Perhaps it is true to say that our very economy is actually driven by moments of inspiration and conclusion that have occurred in moments of forced immobility and natural distraction.

We will never know for certain if such is an objective truth since few would admit that their times of enlightenment have happened with trousers [or skirts] around their ankles and a copy of The Daily Blurb resting on their bony knees.

Most would claim such moments of truth arrive during board meetings – or should they be called 'bored at meetings'? – or during the rushed tube journey homeward.

But it is with conviction that I declare this nonsense.

The toilet is the English persons' equivalent of Buddhas' Banyan tree.

It is here that insight occurs and the enforced calming of the logical brain by natures dictates permits the right brain to practice its' latent creativity.

One could say that genius is born in the bog!

I am unaware of any specific studies that have been undertaken in this particular regard but if one was to hazard a guess at the time spent reading favourite books, comics and newspapers or considering the very meaning of life whilst sat on the domestic or industrial throne it would certainly be hugely significant.

For this very reason I decided one early morning a few weeks ago whilst contemplating my toes and the merits of a high fibre diet that a book containing an element of thoughtfulness, novelty and humour might be just the ticket for the 2004 'bog hogger' and provide those interested segments of the reading population with an upmarket piece of well-written English literature of the light hearted kind that would nevertheless offer a catalyst for thought generation and inventiveness.

Behold the creation of *'The Quintessential Bathroom Companion'*.

As you reflect upon the 424 quirky proverbs and enjoy the various images supplied by Thomas Crapper & Co. Ltd herein may I wish you all happy reading and many hours of comfortable cogitation as well as an excuse to escape from the rest of the family, friends colleagues and the challenges of the wider world.

Should you be inspired to buy anything you actually cast your eyes upon as far as toilet seats, cisterns and other items of useful bathroom application are concerned then please do contact **Thomas Crapper & Co. Ltd** – established 1861 and still going strong - for further information.

A

1. *Advice that is unwanted is about as useful as a chocolate teapot when the Vicar comes around for afternoon tea.*

   [Advice whispered is worthless.]

2. *A straight snooker cue is crooked in another mans' pint of beer.*

   [A straight stick is crooked in the water.]

3. *An army of rabbits led by a ferret would be more formidable than an army of ferrets led by a rabbit.*

   [An army of stags led by a lion would be more formidable than one of lions led by a stag.]

4. *A good face is a letter of recommendation whereas a bad one is like a council tax bill.*

   [A good face is a letter of recommendation.]

5. *A beautiful woman without virtue is like a pint of beer with soggy peanuts in it.*

   [A fair woman without virtue is like stale wine.]

6. *All coalminers are grey in the dark. Mind you, they are in the daylight too.*

   [All cats are grey in the dark.]

7. *A man in debt is like a acne- encrusted teenager; confused and with no immediate remedy.*

   [A man in debt is trapped in a net.]

8. *A quiet conscience sleeps through the barking of a hungry Pit Bull Terrier with a thorn in its' paw.*

   [A quiet conscience sleeps through thunder.]

9. *A pig that is stuck in the mud will tell other pigs he is stuck in chocolate.*

   [A hog that's bemired will endeavour to bemire others.]

10. *An old salesman or an attractive Avon Lady is not easily turned away.*

    [An old fox is not easily snared.]

11. *A false tongue is, surprisingly, not as rare as a set of false teeth.*

    [A false tongue will hardly speak truth.]

12. *All roads lead to Barnsley and this can sometimes be frustrating if trying to travel somewhere else..*

    [All roads lead to Rome.]

13. *All work and little pay makes Jack inclined to go on strike.*

    [All work and no play makes Jack a dull boy.]

14. *An apple-pie without some cheese is like a snog without a squeeze.*

    [Traditional]

15. *An Englishmans' home is anything he can afford to buy in these challenging times of inflated property prices and inadequate salaries.*

    [An Englishman's home is his castle.]

16. *An ounce of practice used to be worth a pound of precept but now a gram of the former is worth a kilogram of the latter and is, although confusing and requiring a fair understanding of mathematics and the principles of conversion formulae, far more valuable.*

[An ounce of practice is worth a pound of precept.]

17. *At the end of the meal there is seldom any curried king prawn to put back into the bag.*

[At the end of the game the king and the pawn go into the same bag.]

18. *A friend in the market will often be chilled to the bone and will tend to wear fingerless mittens and have a blue nose.*

[A friend in the market is better than money in the chest.]

19. *A lazy sheep thinks that its' wool is too heavy.*

[Traditional]

20. *All is fair in love and darts.*

[All is fair in love and war]

21. *A deaf husband and a blind wife are always a happy couple.*

[Traditional]

22. *A builder in a frosted English ditch could never guess what he might do in the heat of passion.nor, generally, would he be able.*

[No man can guess in cold blood what he may do in a passion.]

23. *An Englishman is never happy unless he is free to grumble.*

   [Traditional]]

24. *A cat wearing gloves finds it hard to catch a mouse wearing training shoes.*

   [A cat in gloves catches no mice.]

25. *After all is said and done, more is said than done.*

   [The proverb of a Debating Society member.]

26. *An English womans' sword is her tongue and she will never, ever let it rust.*

   [Traditional]

27. *A bucket with a hole in its base will hold water better than an English womans' mouth can a secret.*

   [Traditional.]

28. *All too often a clear conscience is merely the result of a bad memory.*

   [Traditional]

29. *Age is all in the mind; the real challenge is to keep it from creeping down into the body.*

   [Traditional]

30. *All's well that ends well unless it involves six pints of Old Enochs' Premium Ale. Then it will end exceptionally well but begin very badly the next day.*

[Very traditional and often repeated.]

ℬ

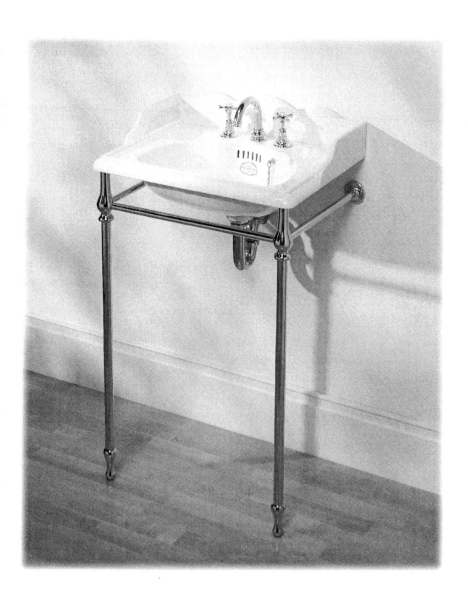

31. *Blessed is he who expects very few crisps in his packet for he shall never be disappointed.*

   [Blessed is he that expects nothing for he shall never be disappointed.]

32. *Believe nothing of what you hear and only half of what you see and especially when it comes to purchasing a second hand car or a German Shepherd Dog in the local pub.*

   [Believe nothing of what you hear and only half of what you see.]

33. *Bold men have generous hearts but they can still fail if the bold men have diets too high in salt, sugar and saturated fats.*

   [Bold men have generous hearts.]

34. *Bullies are always cowards and they often have their eyes placed a little too close together.*

   [Bullies are always cowards.]

35. *Better to give a naan bread than to lend and lose a whole curry supper.*

   [Better give a shilling than lend and lose half a crown.]

36. *Better a belly burst than good chocolates go to waste.*

   [Better belly burst than good meat lost.]

37. *Better to say that you found the trinket that was in your coat pocket on the footpath than tell your wife about the one-eyed barmaid you bestowed with gratitude after she served you your seventh pint of the evening and whose garter you had decided to keep for posterity.*

   [Better a lie that heals than a truth that wounds.]

38. *Better is a woman late if buying the drinks than early without her purse.*

[Better late if ripe and bear than early blossom and blast.]

39. *Bad customs are like good Battenburg cake; better broken and disposed of quickly and not forgetting the crumbs.*

[Bad customs is like good cake, better broken than kept.]

40. *Better to date a bad tempered Rottveiler wearing lipstick than a woman when the moon is full.*

[Sort of traditional}

41. *Better to be half hanged, soaking wet, lost, lonely, and suffering from terrible feverish delusions, ravaged with endless productive bouts of coughing and extreme tiredness, in the middle of a dark winters night without socks and with no money for a bag of chips than be unhappily married.*

[Better to be half hanged than to be ill wed.]

42. *Blood is thicker than water but certainly not than Old Ebeneezers' Brewers Droop Xmas Ale.*

[Blood is thicker than water.]

43. *Behind every successful English man is an astonished English wife.*

[Behind every successful man is a great wife.]

44. *Better the chippy you know than the chippy you don't know.*

[Better the devil you know than the devil you don't know.]

45. *Birds can sing with broken wings but you cant pull feathers off frogs.*

[It may well be traditional but what on earth does it mean?]

46. *Bends in the road do not necessarily mark the end of the road unless you fail to change direction..*

[Traditional]

47. *Bad news travels fast and especially if our neighbour with the curlers from No.102 has anything to do with it.*

[Bad news travels fast.]

48. *Beware of geeks bearing gifts.*
    In fact beware of geeks – period.

[Beware of Greeks bearing gifts.]

49. *Beware a man carrying a ladder, he could be a window cleaner who will ask for your money, a burglar who will take your money or a builder who already has most of your money.*

[M. A. Lee 2004]

50. *"Barking dogs seldom bite" they say.*
    They haven't met my Uncle Zachs' Alsatian , Jake. He does.

[Barking dogs seldom bite]

51. *Buses are vehicles that run twice as fast when you are after them than when you are in them.*

[Traditional.]

52. *Blowing up a goose with dynamite brings no meat to the hunter but may bring the police to the hunters house.*

[M. A. Lee 2004]

53. *Be kind to people on the way up, you may need their help on the way down.*

[A variation of the proverb below]

54. *Bad workmen blame their pals and so do good workmen.*

[Bad workmen blame their tools.]

55. *Bankers are people who lend you their umbrellas when the sun is shining and want them back the minute it begins to rain.*

[Sad but truly traditional.]

56. *Best friends are like four-leaved clovers; hard to find but lucky to have.*

[Traditional]

57. *Be careful whose toes you tread on; they might be attached to the legs of someone whose arse you will need to kiss at a later date.*

[A variation of the proverb above.]

58. *Better to meet a drunkard robbed of his beer than a fool in a position of management.*

[Better meet a bear robbed of his cubs than a fool in his folly.]

59. *Beware the appearance of a man with a bill; it may actually be a duck with a hat on.*

[Ancient.]

C

60. *Children have wide ears and long tongues and especially those who live in the vicinity of nuclear power stations.*
Sometimes, it is said, they also have webbed feet and an extra finger or two.

[Children have wide ears and long tongues.]

61. *Cut off your nose to spite your face and you can guarantee a trip to the local hospital casualty department and the probable loss of your sense of smell.*

[Cut off your nose to spite your face.]

62. *Cold hands, no gloves.*

[Cold hands, warm heart.]

63. *Charity begins at home and usually ends abruptly when some over zealous nuisance in the middle of the town shakes a tin can in your face.*

[Charity begins at home.]

64. *Common sense is the least common of the senses.*

[Traditional]

65. *Children grow by leaps and bounds and often with loud yells and much screeching and this is especially true in the terrace house next to ours.*

[Children grow by leaps and bounds.]

66. *Conscience is the inner voice that warns us someone may be looking.*

[Traditional]

67. *Change your dwelling place often or you will find yourself decorating yet again..*

[Change your dwelling place often for the sweetness in life consists of variety.]

68. *Choose not your underwear by candlelight or you will go to work dressed in a similar fashion to your wife..*

[Choose neither women nor linen by candlelight.]

69. *Cheat once at Snakes and Ladders and you will cheat a thousand times at almost everything else.*

[M. A. Lee 2004]

70. *Compromise is the art of dividing a cake so that everyone thinks he has got the biggest slice.*

[The proverb of a tactful company Director.]

71. *Curses, like grown up children who are unemployed and without accommodation,, come home to roost.*

[Curses, like chickens, come home to roost.]

72. *Canned laughter cannot be bought at the supermarket and neither can a barrel of laughs.*

[M. A. Lee 2004]

73. *Choose a wife by your ear rather than by your eye.*

[Traditional]

74. *Content is even more than a Special Haddock with chips and bits after an evening at the bingo.*

[Content is more than a kingdom.]

75. *Children may pluck apples from trees that Grandfathers planted.*

[Traditional]

76. *Coming events, like North bound traction engines on a sunny afternoon, cast their shadows before them.*

[Coming events cast their shadows before them.]

77. *Curiosity didn't kill the cat; it was the 4.50 express to Kings Cross. If there weren't rats living near the railway tracks it would never have happened.*

[Curiosity killed the cat.]

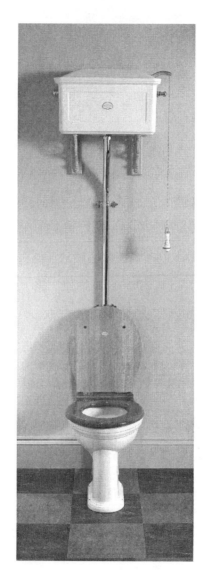

78. *Don't bargain for fish that are still in the midst of the chippys' deep fat fryer.*

[Don't bargain for fish that are still in the water.]

79. *Distance often lends enchantment to the view but certainly not when it comes to Old Aunty Agnes' giant bloomers hung out on the washing line.*

[Distance lends enchantment to the view]

80. *Do not use a hatchet to remove a fly from a friends' forehead.*

[The proverb of a High Street Butcher.]

81. *Don't make love at the garden gate, love is blind but the neighbours aint.*

[Traditional]

82. *Don't put new wine into old bottles; pour it into your mouth and savour it.*

[Don't put new wine into old bottles]

83. *Discretion is the better part of valour; the other but nevertheless still important part is a clean pair of underpants and fresh armpits.*

[Discretion is the better part of valour.]

84. *Don't count the days but rather make the days count.*

[Traditional]

85. *Diligence may well be the Mother of good fortune but Prudence who lives at number 13 on our estate is the Mother of eleven children.*

[Diligence is the Mother of good fortune.]

86. *Desperate diseases may well call for desperate remedies but bleach, after shave or undiluted weed killer in whatever quantities will never reverse the result of Saturday night indiscretions.*

[Desperate diseases call for desperate measures.]

87. *Don't burn your bridges behind you; the police will arrest you and you will be convicted of arson.*

[Don't burn your bridges behind you.]

88. *Don't keep a dog and bark yourself; the dog will probably run away and few friends will want to spend time with you.*

[Don't keep a dog and bark yourself.]

89. *Do unto others as you would have them do unto you but ask first and especially the blonde air hostess at the bar who has never spoken to you before.*

[Do unto others as you would have them do unto you.]

90. *Don't count your chickens before they are hatched and neither count the chickens of your neighbour, cousin or local farmer before they're hatched either. The former is a waste of time and the latter may well involve trespassing on their land and breaking into their hen huts.*

[Don't count your chickens before they're hatched.]

91. *Don't let the Bastards grind you down.*

[From the ancient Yorkshire-Latinesque phrase 'Non carburundum illigitematum']

92. *Don't teach your Grandmother to suck eggs; she certainly wouldn't appreciate such useless tuition and she may well clatter you with her walking stick.*

   [Don't teach your Grandmother to suck eggs.]

93. *Don't wait for your ship to come in; swim out to it. If you cant swim borrow a rowing boat.*

   [The first sentence is traditional]

94. *Definition of certain English Builders' estimates: a sum of money equal to half the final cost and a time for completion a year earlier than actually realized.*

   [M. A. Lee 2004]

95. *Definition of an English expert; a man who comes from more than 20 miles away but not from an adjacent county.*

   [M. A. Lee 2004]

96. *Dictionaries and imagination are the only places where success comes before work.*

   [Dictionaries are the only places where success comes before work.]

97. *Don't spoil the garden hut for want of a fivers' worth of wood stain.*

   [Don't spoil the ship for a ha'porth of tar.]

98. *Drunkenness does not produce faults, it discovers them and so it is always worth keeping your wardrobe locked after a session at the pub.*

   [Drunkenness does not produce faults; it discovers them.]

99. *Deeds are like tasty chocolate truffles but words are but silver wrappers.*

[Deeds are like fruit but words are but leaves.]

100. *Do not let what you cannot do interfere with what you can do with the exception of bar billiards and welly throwing competitions.*

[Do not let what you cannot do interfere with what you can do.].]

101. *Dally not near a furious woman wearing horn-rimmed glasses but rather head for the hills and quickly..*

[M. A. Lee 2004.]

E

102. *Every man wants a ferret run four feet longer than the one he has got.*

[Every man wants a boat four feet longer than the one he has got.]

103. *Even good news can be bad news if it's false or presented by a man with a giant gobstopper is his mouth.*

[Even good news is bad news if it's false.]

104. *Enthusiasm is like a Pit Bull Terrier; it needs regular and abundant feeding but it also needs a strong tether.*

[Enthusiasm is like a fire; it needs feeding and watching.]

105. *Experience is not what happens to an English man; it is what an English man does with what has happened to him.*

[Traditional]

106. *Everyone can make a mistake but not everyone can make a model steam engine from matchsticks like my Uncle John in Wakefield Prison.*

[Everyone can make a mistake but to repeat it is stupidity.]

107. *Even ugly faces are worth looking at and this is indeed a great comfort for most people in the area of Huddersfield where I live..*

[Semi-traditional.]

108. *Even when an English woman is as shy as a mouse you still have to beware of the tiger within.*

[Traditional.]

109. *Empty beer barrels and insignificant people always make the most noise.*

[Traditional.]

110. *Everything has an end except a sausage – and that has two.*

[Always useful to know such things.]

111. *Even a genius cannot seem to meet his Mother-In-Law when he is well dressed.*

[A fact of life!]

112. *Evening promises made to a pretty girl are like butter; as the morning sun rises they all tend to melt away.*

[Traditional.]

113. *Eat a toad in the early morning and nothing worse can possibly happen to you during the rest of the day.*

[Traditional in unusual parts of Yorkshire.]

114. *Every beggar is descended from some king and every king is descended from some beggar.*
This is a comforting philosophy for a beggar but not at all for a king.

[Traditional]

115. *Even a skilled hand cannot pick two nostrils at the same time.*

[Even a skilled hand cannot sew with two needles at the same time.]

116. *Everything is hard in the beginning and, if not, there is always medication.*

[Everything is hard in the beginning.]

117. *Even if the chef at our pub deep-fried a fly he would keep the breast for himself.*

[Traditional]

118. *Even good dogs have fleas and, incidentally, so does my Uncle Amos.*

[Even good dogs have fleas.]

119. *Even a nightingale will run out of songs before an English woman runs out of conversation.*

[Traditional.]

120. *Experience is certainly the Father of Wisdom but no-one knows who the Father of the small boy at the end of our road happens to be.*

[Experience is the Father of wisdom.]

121. *Eyes should both be wide open before marriage and only one closed afterwards.*

[Traditional but sometimes forgotten.]

F

122. *Fact is stranger than fiction and no more evident than in certain villages to the North of Halifax.*

[Fact is stranger than fiction.]

123. *Familiarity may well breed contempt but Rita Cleggs' family breeds award winning ferrets.*

[Familiarity breeds contempt.]

124. *Far fetched and dear bought is good for many English ladies.*

[Traditional.]

125. *For a trip, choose good companions, for a home, choose good neighbours.*

[Traditionally sensible.]

126. *Fools rush in where Hell's Angels fear to tread.*

[Fools rush in where angels fear to tread.]

127. *Flies on top of pylons think that they are taller than pylons.*

[Traditionally puzzling.]

128. *Forty is the old age of youth and fifty the youth of old age.*

[A traditional proverb cited by forty and fifty year old English folk.]

129. *Fish are no respecters of human boredom so why on earth bother with fishing?*

[Traditionally fishy.]

130. *Finding a friend or neighbour with your wife on your sofa means that it is time to sell your sofa.*

[Traditionally quirky.]

131. *Finding and allocating blame to The French can be far more interesting to many English folk than football, sex and bingo.*
Bingo, of course, is a close second!

[M. A. Lee 2004]

132. *Fields have eyes and woods have ears especially to the man who consumes a half a gallon of Old Gutter Huggers Dark Ale.*

[Fiends have eyes and woods have ears.]

133. *For a river to freeze three feet deep it takes more than one day of cold weather.*

[Traditionally cryptic.]

134. *Flowing water doesn't stink and stinking water doesn't flow.*

[Traditionally poignant or should it be pungent?]

135. *Friendship is a plant that must be watered regularly.*

[Traditionally educational.]

136. *Fortune may one day turn against you and then even jelly will break your teeth.*

[Traditionally worrying]

137. *Finding a diamond with a few small flaws is better than finding a perfect rock.*

[Traditionally unlikely.]

138. *Fish and house guests are rather similar; they both become unsavoury and unwanted after they've been around for three days or more.*

[Traditionally and often experienced.]

139. *Frugality that leads to extravagance is often seen, extravagance to frugality is not.*

[Traditionally observed]

140. *Frogs may well be seated on golden stools but they will soon jump of them into the marsh from which they first emerged.*

[Traditionally fantastical.]

141. *For a dwarf there are giants everywhere and for a giant the world is full of dwarves.*

[A traditional proverb of variable dimensions.]

142. *Friends in need are friends that are not always so popular.*

[A friend in need is a friend indeed.]

143. *For true wisdom take nine parts of silence and one part of few words.*

[Not at all traditional in the majority of English towns and villages.]

144. *Friends of the Captain can wipe their hands on the sail.*

[The proverb of a Seafarers' friend who took things just a little too far.]

G

145. *God may well help those who help themselves in matters of application but certainly not in taking sweets from Woolworths' pick and mix counter without paying.*

[God helps those who help themselves.]

146. *Goodwill makes the road shorter, the council makes the road uneven.*

[Goodwill makes the road shorter.]

147. *Gentlemen don't want to give much and are ashamed to give little. Most English men don't want to give much and are proud to give nothing.*

[The first sentence is traditional, the second merely true.]

148. *Grain by grain, a loaf; matchstick by matchstick, a model traction engine.*

[Grain by grain, a loaf; stone by stone, a castle.]

149. *Gardeners with little skill argue with their rakes. [My Uncle Jacob does; I've heard him!]*

[Traditional - or at least as far as the first part is concerned]

150. *Go to a large river to find a large fish but be prepared to be soaked in the process.*

[A word of caution to the bravest of fishermen and chip shop owners.]

151. *Grasp today with both hands because yesterday is but a dream and tomorrow is barely a vision.*

[The proverb of a Film Producer.]

152. *Geese may well be worth twenty pounds each but to catch one you must first spend a fiver for a catapult and some marbles.*

[A traditional English Poachers' comment about business investment.]

153. *Gardeners who love roses are slaves to a thousand thorns.*

[Traditional.]

154. *Gossip is one item that travels without the need for a postage stamp.*

[Scandalous but true and interesting to know that my neighbour with the curlers at No.102 told me so.]

155. *Gardens without fences are like dogs without tails.*

[Flies and neighbours children are very similar in their tendency to unwanted invasion.]

156. *Give to me a joke and I will show you the hole through which the truth whistles.*

[Rumoured to be an ancient Cavers proverb.]

157. *Gallows made of gold are no good at all if you about to be hung on them.*

[Traditional]

158. *Good luck generally comes in half pint glasses but bad luck in one hundred gallon barrels.*

[A traditional English Landlords' comment about business returns.]

159. *Growing is something you have to do on your own even if your Grandfather was a giant.*

[The proverb of a Personal Development Manager.]

160. *Good clients don't change shops in three years and good shops don't change clients for three years.*

[A traditional English Shopkeepers comment about business database forecasting given that he/she is about to change his/her business concerns during the fourth year.]

161. *Getting a chicken back into an egg is easier than undoing slanderous gossip.*

[A traditional English farmers' comment about the difficulties he faced whilst attempting to restore his soiled reputation having been rumoured to water down his milk before bottling.]

162. *Give a dog a tasty name and eat him.*

[The proverb of a rather obsessive English Survival Expert regards the alternative means to eating when business is not going too well and restaurant prices are too high.]

163. *Govern a family as you would cook a small fish..*

[A traditional Chefs' comment hopefully based on culinary techniques that <u>do not</u> involve battering and deep frying.]

164. *Great things can be reduced to small things and small things can be reduced to nothing and especially when it comes to bank accounts and an over ambitious wife.*

[A traditional English husbands' comment about his beloveds spending inclinations.]

165. *Genius can be recognized by its' childish simplicity.*

[A traditional Yorkshire Authors' comment on his raison d'etre and a plea for recognition.]

H

166. He who rides upon an ass cannot help but smell its' gas.

[The proverb of an English Equestrian.]

167. He that counts the crisps of a friend is a man for whom a seat at the bar is rarely reserved..

[He that counts a mans mistakes will be abandoned.]

168. However fast a man might be he can never outrun his shadow. However cunning a man might be he can never pacify his wife. However thorough a man might be he can never kill all his garden slugs.

[If a man tells you otherwise he is, according to Whitby tradition, an unmitigated liar.]

169. He who thinks too much about every step he takes will stay on one leg all his life.

[Traditional]

170. He who doesn't like chattering women must remain a bachelor.

[There is reputedly a village to the North of Scunthorpe where this is not so but I am unable to find the place.]

171. Hang your hat higher than you can reach and sooner or later you will fall off the step ladders.

[Don't hang your hat higher than you can reach.]

172. Hunchbacks can see the humps of others but never their own.

[A traditional Opticians saying.]

173. *He who chatters with you will chatter about you.*

[So my neighbour with the curlers at Number 102 tells me!]

174. *He who gets a name for early rising can stay in bed until midday.*

[The proverb of someone employed in the Advertising Industry.]

175. *He who is dependant on others must make friends with his ferret.*

[Traditional Doncaster proverb.]

176. *He who tickles himself can laugh whenever he wants.*

[A very sad proverb from The Essex Traction Engine & Tea Dance Society]

177. *He that marries a widow will often have a dead mans head thrown in his dish.*

[Traditional and rather worrying if true.
It is said by many widows in certain pit villages to the South of Barnsley that widows in various pit villages to the North of Barnsley keep the decapitated heads of their husbands in their pantries, bringing them out for show only on special occasions.]

178. *Hear all, see all, say nowt;*
    Eat all, sup all, say nowt;
    And if thou ever does owt for nowt allus' do it for thysen.

[The ultimate and best known of all Yorkshire proverbs]

179. *Hell hath no fury like a woman with chip grease spilled on her best blouse.*

[Hell hath no fury like a woman scorned]

180. *Hope for the best and prepare for the worst especially when visiting certain towns and villages in the West Midlands.*

[A traditional proverb rarely recited by residents of certain towns and villages in the West Midlands but often recited by other people who don't happen to live there.]

181. *How sweet it is to hear ones' own convictions from a strangers' mouth.*

[A proverb credited to Goethe who is said to have learned it from a Selby man.]

182. *How reassuring to know that old age will always be twenty years older than I happen to be..*

[A traditional Optimists' proverb.]

183. *History repeats itself like a late-night donor kebab with chilli sauce; it involves notably uncomfortable lessons and each time the price is higher.*

[History is always repeating itself but each time the price goes up.]

I

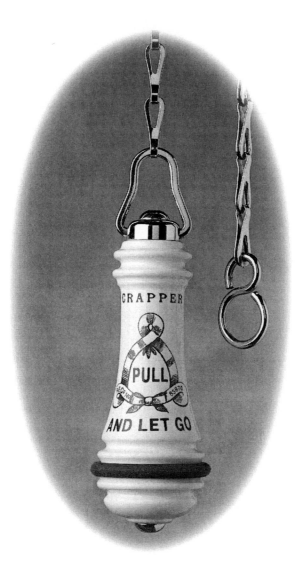

184. *It isn't the actual job that takes the time; it's the starting and the finishing of it.*

[A traditional English Office Workers' excuse for not completing a task on time.]

185. *If you don't want your children to hear what you're saying pretend that you are talking to them.*

[The proverb of a Parent.]

186. *It costs nothing to guess, but to guess wrongly can be very costly indeed.*

[The proverb of a Gambler.]

187. *If a man deceives me once then shame on him; if he deceives me twice, then shame on me.*

[A traditional Monday Market Shoppers' lament.]

188. *In the wondrous world of analogues skating on thin ice can sometimes get you into hot water.*

[A traditional Wordsmiths' confusion of circumstances.]

189. *If you get a good wife you will be happy; if you get a bad one you will become a Philosopher.*

[A traditional English Philosophers' saying.]

190. *In the land of the blind the one eyed man often goes travelling and is rarely convicted of theft.*

[A traditional one-eyed English mans' comment on life as it actually is in a small East End neighbourhood.]

191. *I pointed out to you the stars and yet all you saw was the tip of my finger.*

[A traditional and overly keen Fathers' frustrated reprimand of his astronomically disinterested three month old Son.]

192. *Ignorance is the Mother of Impudence.*

[Two women's names traditionally said in Yorkshire to be commonly found in villages within Lancashire.]

193. *It is difficult to catch a black cat in a dark room and especially when it is not there.*

[A traditional Mystics' thought for the day.]

194. *If your enemy wrongs you, buy each of his children a drum.*

[The proverb of an experienced Tactician.]

195. *If a flea had money it would buy its' own dog.*

[If a flea could write this would be its' favourite proverb]

196. *It is a bold mouse that makes its' nest in a cats' ear.*

[A traditional Pet Shop Owners sales pitch as he tries to sell a mouse with strange behavioural problems.]

197. *Ignorance doesn't necessarily kill you but it certainly makes you sweat a lot.*

[Traditional.]

198. *In a tree that you cant climb there are always a thousand fruits.*

[A traditional schoolboys' lament.]

199. *'If' married 'But' and their child was called ' Maybe'.*

[In a village close to Halifax these are said to be real people and their shortage of excuses knows no end!]

200. *If it rained macaroni, what a great time would be had by gluttons everywhere.*

[A traditional proverb written by an obese English man who visited Italy.]

201. *If you wake up in the morning and feel no pain or stiffness it is possible that you died in the night.*

[A traditional Octogenarians' everyday observation.]

202. *In the eyes of a lover a pock marked face is one with pretty dimples.*

[In certain parts of England and especially those close to ancient Plague Villages this is often just as well.]

203. *If the hill is on fire the grasshoppers are roasted.*

[Traditionally certain.]

204. *Idleness moves so slowly that it is generally overtaken by misery.*

[A proverb that is so sad that it should be read quickly.]

205. *It is as difficult to win love as it is to pack salt in pine needles.*

[A traditional Salt Packers' saying.]

206. *I may not be best butter but I'm on your side of the bread.*

[*Originally said by a lady from Basingstoke called 'Marj'.*]

J

THOS. CRAPPER & Co.,
Ltd.,

Sanitary Engineers

TO

His Majesty the King

AND

H.R.H. The Prince of Wales.

BY APPOINTMENT.

BY APPOINTMENT.

BATHS, LAVATORIES, SINKS, &c.

Show Rooms :

120, KING'S ROAD, CHELSEA, S.W.

(OPPOSITE ROYAL AVENUE.)

Here is a wonderful picture of the Show Rooms of the early Thomas Crapper & Co. Ltd based in Chelsea.

Today the company is to be found at The Stable Yard, Alscot Park, Stratford-On-Avon in Warwickshire CV37 8BL.

207. *Judgement should not be passed on a man until the judge and every member of the jury has walked a mile in his clogs.*

[Before I pass judgement on a man let me walk a mile in his moccasins.]

208. *Judge a society by the way it treats its' Gypsies.*

[The proverb of an English Gypsy.]

209. *Judge the linen by the hem and a girl by her mother.*

[The advice of a Textile worker to his single apprentice.]

210. *Jam tomorrow and jam yesterday but today we eat beef dripping on bread.*

[The original Bingley proverb from which, it is rumoured, Lewis Carroll derived his proverb for the book *'Alice Through The Looking Glass;'* The rule is - jam tomorrow and jam yesterday but never jam today.']

K

211. *Know which side your bread is buttered and hope that it doesn't fall butter side down into the dog basket.*

[Know which side your bread is buttered.]

212. *Kindness is like the seed of Pennine cotton grass; the more one sows the more it grows.*

[A traditional Conservationists proverb.]

213. *Kindness is the music to which the one legged man can dance.*

[Kindness is the language that the deaf can hear and the blind can read.]

214. *Kindle not a fire you cannot put out unless you are a mill owner and your mill is no longer providing a profitable business.*

[Reputedly a traditional Yorkshire Loss Adjusters satirical comment on the misfortune of apparently spontaneous fires in the once great Northern textile industry.]

215. *Kennels containing hungry dogs are no places to keep sausages.*

[The proverb of a Meat Wholesaler.]

216. *Kings may well make knights but they rarely, if ever, make Yorkshire puddings.*

[Kings make knights but not gentlemen.]

217. *Knowledge is like a gooseberry; it is sweet and flavoursome but must first be picked from a thorny and unforgiving bush.*

[Knowledge has bitter roots but sweet fruits.]

218. *Knowledge may well make an English man smile but finding a pound coin under a settee cushion will make an English man dance.*

[Knowledge makes one laugh but wealth makes one dance.]

219. *Kill not the goose that lays the golden egg but rather contact a National Newspaper immediately. Reporters tend to pay small fortunes for stories of unusual phenomena like this.*

[Kill not the goose that lays the golden egg.]

220. *Keepers of fat bellies are never the same as owners of sharp minds.*

[A fat belly does not breed a subtle mind.]

221. *Kick a big man when he is down and you had better invest in a pair of running shoes for when he gets up again.*

[M. A. Lee 2004]

222. *Knowledge is like an allotment; if it isn't cultivated there can be no harvest.*

[A proverb from Surrey.]

223. *Keep your eyes wide open before marriage and only half shut afterwards.*

[Traditional in all parts of England and beyond.]

224. *Keep a thing for seven years and you will find a use for it.*

[The exceptions to these words of great wisdom are lame ferrets, broken vases and empty, disposable biro pens although not, apparently, in Huddersfield.]

225. *Know this and never forget it; women are saints in church, angels in the street and devils in the home. Be careful where you first meet them!*

[Said to be first written by the Cornish Saint, Old Herbert the Very Astute.]

226. *Knowledge is a possession no one can rob you of and a tattered baseball cap is a possession no-one would want to rob you of.*

[Written by a rather knowledgeable man who always wore an old baseball cap.]

227. *Kiss a thief and you had better count your teeth again.*

[Written by the wife of a Hull Prison inmate.]

228. *Knives that are licked soon cut tongues.*

[Originated after the 1995 Sheffield teenager cult fashion of sharp knife licking and said to have been written by a learned doctor in Accident and Emergency Medicine.]

229. *Kid a kidder, con a con man but never try to mislead an English man.*

[M. A. Lee 2004]

230. *Ketchup's good with sausages, ketchup's good with chips, ketchup's good with everything and is plastered all over my lips.*

[The recent though soon to be traditional proverb of a 7 year old Yorkshire boy.]

L

231. *Laugh and the world laughs with you, cry and only you and the drunk in the corner of the bar will cry together. He would cry even if you didn't.*

[Laugh and the world laughs with you, cry and you cry alone.]

232. *Laughter is the best medicine followed as a close second by Old Cyrils' Special Brew.*

[Laughter is the best medicine]

233. *Laughter is the closest distance between two people.*

[First written, or so it is said, by a specialist in Geometry at a Hampshire Secondary School.]

234. *Learn from the past, live for today, look to tomorrow and take a nap this afternoon.*

[A proverb said to originate from the village of Great Slumber.]

235. *Life is a mystery to be lived not a problem to be solved.*

[This proverb is said to be one first coined by an English Philosopher with an eye for pragmatism.]

236. *Life is like a dart board; it can be a great game unless a dart lands in your eye.*

[Written by a one-eyed man who used to play darts.]

237. *Life is like a greyhound race; there are winners and there are losers and many of the contenders are barking.*

[Life is like a horse race; there are winners and there are losers.]

238. *Like the measles, love is most dangerous when it comes late in life.*

[Written by a man after he had recovered from the rash and high temperature that inspired his unfortunate interest in the one legged, twenty five stone lady that worked in theLancashire chip shop.]

239. *Lack of planning on your part does not constitute an emergency on my part.*

[The proverb of a privately owned Breakdown Service Provider called out to a car that has run out of petrol.]

240. *Love starts with a smile, grows with a kiss and ends with triplets.*

[In some places love starts with a smile, grows with a kiss and ends with tears. This is rarely the case in parts of Seacroft near Leeds.]

241. *Leopards do not change their spots nor does my great Aunt Enid change her underwear.*

[Leopards do not change their spots.]

242. *Learn to say 'No'. This is far more useful than learning Latin or Algebra.*

[A proverb often recited by a Mother of twelve from Rotherham who, to this very day, wonders why she can recite the poems of the Roman, Catullus, and forecast the trajectory of comets but is unable to shake off her tendency to agree to everything suggested in the romantic department.]

243. *Lose an hour in the morning and you will likely spend all day looking for it.*

[This happens a great deal close to the border with Scotland but tends to involve pennies rather than hours.]

244. *Love many, trust few and always paddle your own canoe.*

[Allegedly contrived by the Rev J. Wigfield in 1978]

245. *Long and lazy, little and loud, fat and fulsome, pretty and proud.*

[The four types of women often seen in Wakefield.]

246. *Life is short and the future is uncertain so if you want a kebab have a kebab.*

[Life is short and the future is uncertain therefore don't waste opportunities.]

247. *Lots of people confuse bad management with destiny.*

[That's just the way it is!]

248. *Let it be said that I would rather have a friend in my tent spitting outside than I would a friend outside spitting in.*

[The proverb of a Camper with an odd view of acceptable outdoor behaviour.]

249. *Let fools and wind pass.*

[The proverb of a Baked Bean Manufacturer.]

250. *Love is like a mousetrap; you go in when you want but you don't get out when you like.*

[The proverb of a man who was both whiskered and trapped.]

251. *Life is a temporary stop whilst death is the journey home.*

[The proverb of a Bus Driver.]

252. *Lend everyone your ears, give a hand to your friends but give your lips only to a woman.*

[The proverb of a Dealer in body parts.]

253. *Life, like a fire, begins in smoke and ends in ashes.*

[The proverb of an Arsonist.]

254. *Listen to the wisdom of the toothless ones and you will find yourself in Huddersfield for a lifetime.*

[The original version ' Listen to the wisdom of the toothless ones' is said to be the proverb of a Dentist.]

255. *Life is like perpetual drunkenness; the pleasure passes but the headache remains.*

[The proverb of the publican that owns 'The Wilted Rose and The Balding Crown' in the ancient village of Old Gimmersdale.]

257. *Many a true word is spoken in jest.*

[The proverb of a Comedian.]

258. *Middle age is when broadness of the mind and narrowness of the waist change places.*

[A proverb attributed to a member of the Warwickshire Weight Wary Society.]

259. *Muck and money go together.*

[The proverb of a Mangel- wurzel farmer.]

260. *Many hands make light work but may also mean a justified reason to see a geneticist who has a thorough understanding of extra body parts and can advice accordingly.*

[Many hands make light work.]

261. *Moderation in all things including moderation.*

[An immodest English mans' way of justifying yet another jar of evening ale over and above that deemed reasonable and sensible.]

262. *Mills and wives are ever wanting.*

[The proverb of a married Mill Owner]

263. *Marriage halves our griefs, doubles our joys and quadruples our expenses.*

[The proverb of a happily married Accountant.]

264. *Marriage doubles our griefs, halves our joys and quadruples our expenses.*

[The proverb of an unhappily married Accountant.]

265. *Much travel is needed to ripen a mans' rawness.*

[The proverb of an English man who once travelled all the way from Devon to Dorset.]

266. *Men are as old as the women they feel and women as old as they decide they will tell people they are on any given day.*

[Men are as old as they feel and women as old as they look.]

267. *Mother Nature, Time and Patience are the three best doctors. It is difficult to know who are the worst: there are so many to choose from.*

[The first bit is traditional.]

268. *Misers do not own their own gold; it is their gold that owns them.*

[The proverb of a man who was owed gold by a Miser.]

269. *Many men are like clocks; they show one hour and strike another.*

[The proverb of an Horologist.]

270. *Mine and thine are the sources of all quarrels.*

[The proverb of a wise man well versed in the ancient vernacular of South Yorkshire.]

271. *Making money selling manure is better than losing money selling mink coats.*

[The proverb of a Businessman who went bankrupt in the fur trade and was keen to justify his new found occupation.]

272. *Manure is the Farmers' gold.*

[Also attributed to the Businessman of Proverb Number 271 above.]

273. *Mules make a great fuss about their ancestors being donkeys.*

[Traditional and so very like humans!]

274. *Most people like short prayers and long sausages.*

[Long prayers are usually a sign that there is little sausage in the house.]

275. *Mediocrity is climbing molehills without sweating.*

[The proverb of an intolerant and ambitious Mountain Man.]

276. *Merry Nights make sorry days.*

[The proverb of many a hung over English man.]

277. *Men must be lovers of many in their twenties, strong as oxen in their thirties and rich beyond belief in their forties.*

[The proverb of a forty year old Bluffer whose tendency to construct an alternative past and a less than realistic present was well known to all the locals at The Wilting Rose and Balding Crown in Old Gimmersdale.]

278. *Many a man in love with a dimple makes the mistake of marrying the whole girl.*

[The proverb of a man full of regret and faced with far more than a daily dimple.]

279. *Men fall into three classes; the handsome, the intelligent and the majority.*

[The proverb of an observant though cruel English woman.]

The Original Thomas Crapper & Co. Ltd team of bearded Gentlemen and Sanitary Engineers; Thomas Crapper, Robert. M.Wharam & George Crapper. If it were not for them you might be reading this book in the woods!

280. *Nowt so queer as folk and especially when one considers Quentin Dewdrop and his paisley hat from the outskirts of Chelsea.*

[Nowt so queer as folk.]

281. *Never play leapfrog with a unicorn.*

[Thought to have been first voiced by a deluded Yorkshire man who mistook an iron spiked park fence for a creature of legend and returned home from hospital as a Yorkshire woman in considerable discomfort.]

282. *Nothing is certain but death, taxes and delays when travelling by train.*

[The proverb of a Commuter.]

283. *Never stand on the tail of a hedgehog after midnight.*

[The proverb of someone who either once stood on the tail of hedgehog after midnight in the frosty Winter or, at least, knew someone who did.
We are unlikely to discover what exactly happened to this person as a result but I bet it would have made a 'spine-chilling tale'.]

284. *Never do today what you can put off until tomorrow.*

[The original version of 'Never put off until tomorrow what you can do today.']

285. *No one is without knowledge except he who asks no questions.*

[The proverb of a rather sensitive and bitter English man of whom no one had taken any interest.
It is possible that his fixation in train spotting had disadvantaged him somewhat!]

286. *No woman can make a wise man out of a fool but every woman can change a wise man into a fool.*

[The proverb of a monk belonging to The Order of Disillusioned and Runaway Husbands of St Cyril the Withdrawn -Brighton Branch.]

287. *Never set the attic on fire just because you haven't caught any mice.*

[The proverb of a Lancashire Fire Safety Officer.]

288. *No matter how the world changes cats will never lay eggs.*

[A proverb that captures a profound and ancient truth in a subtle and mysterious fashion and is said to have originated in Hereford when a poultry farmer argued over investment possibilities with his cat loving wife.]

289. *Nature has given to us two eyes and two ears but only one mouth so that we may see and hear more than we speak.*

[A proverb often forgotten by gossips across the land and especially our neighbour with the curlers from No.102.]

290. *Necessity can change a pit bull terrier into a poodle..*

[Necessity can change a lion into a fox.]

291. *Never kiss an ugly girl in your village for she will be so grateful for the attention that she will doubtless tell everyone.*

[The same would apply to Quentin Dewdrop of Chelsea but with far worse consequences.]

292. *Never kiss an opportunity with a cold sore on your lips.*

[Never kiss an opportunity with a dirty mouth.]

293. *Never cough if you're hiding in the coal cellar.*

[The proverb of a Cat Burglar who coughed whilst hiding in the coal cellar of Lord & Lady Arbuckle-Plumbmouth of Sheepbridge Castle with a bag full of their silver cutlery and written with great regret within a small Durham Prison cell.]

294. *No matter how many chores you finish in your house there is always yet more to be done.*

[A Housewives' Proverb.]

295. *Nostalgia today is not what is used to be when I was a lad.*

[The proverb of a Satirist.]

O

No. 844

296. One good turn deserves suspicion.

[One good turn deserves another.]

297. Only mad dogs and Englishmen go out in the mid day sun.

[In England itself this tends to occur at the roadside tables of innumerable pubs.]

298. One of these days is none of these days.

[The promise of a certain Builder to return to an improperly completed job.]

299. Only other peoples eggs are double yolked.

[The grass on the other side is always greener.]

300. Opinions are like nails; the often you hit them the deeper they penetrate.

[The proverb of a philosophical Joiner commenting on the views of a headstrong workmate.]

301. Onions, smoke, and women from Kent can all bring tears to your eyes very easily.

[A proverb of observation.]

302. On the ladder to success there is always somebody on the rung above you and who uses your head to steady himself.

[The proverb of a Corporate Climber with a severe headache.]

303. *Of money, wit and virtue believe only a quarter of what you hear. If relating to Huddersfield specifically, believe only one tenth.*

[The proverb of a Cynic.]

304. *Offer a lazy man an egg and he will want you to peel it for him.*

[The proverb of the wife of a slovenly Poultry Farmer.]

305. *Of the good we have an understanding, for fools we keep a large stick upstairs.*

[The proverb of a member of The Barnsley Neighbourhood Lookout Organization with a particular dislike of burglars.]

306. *Old mens' sayings are seldom untrue.*

[Traditional and a proverb to which the Author tips his hat.]

307. *One cannot scoop up the River Humber with an empty cola can..*

[One cannot scoop up the ocean with a seashell.]

308. *One cannot put the clock back but then it shouldn't have been stolen in the first place.*

[One cannot put the clock back.]

309. *Opportunity seldom knocks twice and yet the chap who cleans our wheelie bins seem to knock on our door every other week.*

[A proverb of exception.]

310. *One joy scatters a hundred griefs and one day of pleasure is worth a thousand of sorrow.*

[A well known chat up line that has never been proven to work.]

311. *Our whole life is but a greater and longer childhood.*

[The proverb of a Big Kid.]

312. *One Yorkshire man can beat three Lancastrians.*

[Derived from the saying 'One Englishman can beat three French men'.]

313. *One acre of performance is worth twenty of the land of promise.*

[The proverb of a Sales Manager and his expectation for results.]

314. *One hours' sleep before midnight is worth two afterwards but does require catching an earlier bus back home from town on a Saturday night.*

[One hours sleep before midnight is worth two afterwards.]

P

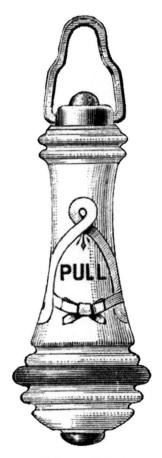

No. 231

315. *People who think that the world revolves around them have no sense of direction.*

[The proverb of an amateur Astronomer who worked for the RAC.]

316. *Promises are like babies; easy to make, hard to deliver.*

[The proverb of a Midwife.]

317. *Patience is a bitter plant but it bears sweet fruit.*

[The proverb of a Gooseberry Grower.]

318. *Parents are patterns and if your Son begins to wear a tartan skirt or your Daughter a paisley trilby you only have yourselves to blame.*

[Parents are patterns.]

319. *Patience is the knot that secures the seam of victory.*

[The proverb of a Tailor.]

320. *Pay peanuts and you will get monkeys; pay with beer and you will end up employing everyone that lives between County Cleveland and Derbyshire.*

[A proverb of likelihood.]

321. *Poverty used to come in at the door and love used to fly out of the window. These days the latter often leaves by the home-based office fire escape!*

[A proverb of changing custom.]

322. *Pride is a weed that grows in the hanging basket.*

[Pride is a flower growing in the devils' garden.]

323. *Promises may make friends but performances keep them.*

[Another proverb of the Sales Manager that we met earlier.]

324. *Proverbs are the children of experience.*

[The proverb of a Genealogist.]

325. *Pick your friends like you pick your nose; with care, caution and consistency.*

[Pick your friends like you pick your fruit.]

326. *Proverbs are like butterflies; some are caught and other fly away.*

[The proverb of my own dear wife regards this endearing collection of English proverbs.
It must be said that she almost never catches butterflies!]

327. *Perseverance is not one single long race; it is a series of short races one after another.*

[The proverb of a Marathon Runner.]

328. *Politeness to human nature is what a microwave oven is to butter.*

[The proverb of a Chef.]

329. *Poverty is a state of mind induced by a neighbours' new conservatory.*

[M. A. Lee 2004.]

330. *People count up the faults of those who keep them waiting..*

[Better never than late.]

331. *Poverty is no disgrace but it is real inconvenience.*

[The proverb of everyone at some time or other.]

332. *Promises, like pie crust, are made to be broken.*

[But not if you buy your pies from Old Mrs Higginbottoms Pie Shop in Knottingley. They cant even be broken with a pneumatic drill. I know; I've tried.]

333. *Providence is always on the side of the man with a petrol lawn mower and rarely on the side of the man with shears.*

[The proverb of a fatalistic Gardener.]

334. *Pen and ink may well be the wits' plough but the word processor is the state of the art combine harvester and, strange as it sounds, even in Scunthorpe these days.*

[Pen and ink are the wits' plough.]

335. *Quality remains long after the price is forgotten..*

[The proverb of Sir Henry Royce, a contemporary of Thomas Crapper.]

336. *Quarrelling dogs often limp home and especially if they are poodles and their opponents are Rottveillers or Pit Bull Terriers.*

[Quarrelling dogs often limp home.]

337. *Quickly come, quickly go.*

[The proverb of a first time visitor to Hartlepool.]

R

338. *Red sky at night, another textile mill has been set alight; red sky in the morning and the Loss Adjusters are yawning.*

[Red sky at night, Shepherds delight; red sky in the morning, Shepherds warning.]

339. *Remorse is the dessert of lust and especially when the latter has been consumed wearing non prescription beer goggles.*

[Remorse is the dessert of lust.]

340. *Revenge never repairs an injury nor does the planning of revenge allow time for the repair of a bicycle tyre.*

[The proverb of a man inclined to forgive, forget and replace his damaged inner tube.]

341. *Rome was not built in a day.*

[The Romans evidently didn't know some of the builders I have had cause to meet over the last few years. They can erect a whole housing estate in under three hours. Granted, the houses are not particularly strong and tend to fall down again within a short period of time but, hey, you cant expect everything can you?]

342. *Rivalry between window cleaners tends to improve the clarity of the view from the lounge into the back garden.*

[Rivalry between scholars improves science.]

343. *Remember that whilst many gardens in villages close to Manchester have only old washing machines and discarded sweet wrappers, in the garden of time there grow flowers of consolation.*

[The proverb of a man who disliked scruffy gardens.]

344. *Rain falls and the grass grows just as beer is served and the conversation follows.*

   [Depending upon the part of England in question the word 'beer' can be replaced by the words 'wine', 'lassi' or ' methylated spirit as appropriate.]

345. *Rudeness is a weak mans imitation of strength.*

   [The proverb of a man who disliked rudeness.]

346. *Rumours are stories that involve more details than the teller heard in the first place.*

   [The proverb of a man who disliked rumours.]

347. *Rich people get richer and poor people get babies.*

   [A traditional proverb from Liverpool.]

348. *Regretting the past is like chasing a dropped orange down the Holme River. Far better to let it go and enjoy a leisurely pint of Old Elis' Promising Future at The Forget It All Tavern.*

   [Rev J. Wigfield 1979.]

349. *Real bad luck is spraining the thumb whilst blowing the nose.*

   [The proverb of a very, very unlucky man who had a cold.]

350. *Real friendship does not freeze in the winter.*
    It is a shame that the same cannot be said of the water pipes in the loft.

   [The proverb of a man who had friendly neighbours but unfriendly plumbing.]

351. *Raw poultry, pets and fish make the churchyards fat.*
So stay away from Blind Freds' café and his Special Stir Fried Cat.

[The first line is traditional if one replaces the word 'pet' with the word ' veal'.]

352. *Reputation is to virtue as good mustard is to sirloin steak.*

[Reputation serves to virtue as light does to a picture.]

353. *Reason governs the wise man and cudgels the fool.*

[A proverb easily understood by some English men and not at all by others.]

S

VALVE CLOSET.

With Basin and Slop Top in one piece, and Ventilating Union off Overflow Trap.

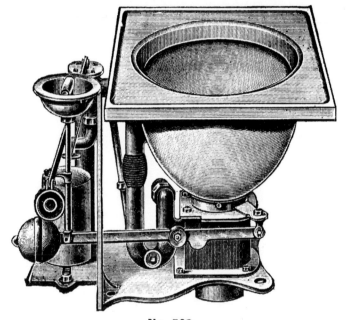

No. 560.

Valve Closet, with White Ware Flushing-rim Basin
with fixed Slop Top, China Dish, 1-in. Supply
Valve, Copper Air Regulator, Ventilating Union
off Trap, complete as shown ... ... **£4 7s. 6d.**

If with 1¼-in. Valve ... ... Extra **3/6**

  ,,   Box Enamelled inside .. ... ,, **4/9**

  ,,   Box fitted with Brass Top ... ,, **6/3**

354. *Seven fifths of all English people do not understand fractions.*

[Or was it eight thirds?]

355. *Smile and the world smiles with you; snore and you sleep alone.*

[The favourite proverb of the Authors' wife.]

356. *Some are Wise and some are Otherwise.*

[A proverb first penned to describe ladies of the WRVS hospital canteens and the spectrum of their mathematical ability regards till and money management.]

357. *Sympathy without relief is like fresh bread without the dripping.*

[Sympathy without relief is like mustard without beef.]

358. *Silence may well be the fence around wisdom but it can also be the fence around deceit, ignorance or plain stupidity.*

[Silence is the fence around wisdom.]

359. *Scandal is like an egg; when it is hatched it has wings.*

[Another proverb from the Poultry Farming Industry.]

360. *Stay where there are songs for bad people don't sing.*

[The proverb of a Folk Club Organizer.]

361. *Soap for the body and tears for the soul.*

[The proverb of an emotional Soap Merchant whose business could have been better.]

362. *Secrets that you keep are your slaves but you become the slave of your secrets if you let them out.*

[The proverb of a Slave who had no secrets left.]

363. *Statistics are like bikinis; what they reveal is interesting but what they conceal is fascinating.*

[The proverb of a Mathematics Teacher on holiday in Majorca.]

364. *Summertime in England consists of three fine days, a thunderstorm and a traction engine rally in the local park.*

[The proverb of a hopeful English man written during the winter months.]

365. *Six hours sleep for a man, seven for a woman and eight for a fool.*

[The proverb of an angry, jealous man whose bad back has led to chronic sleep deprivation and a judgemental attitude.]

366. *Sadness cannot be prevented from flying over ones head from time to time but it can be prevented from nesting in ones hair.*

[The proverb of a bald Razor Salesman.]

367. *Secrets of two no further will go but secrets of three a hundred will know.*

[The proverb of the third party as mentioned above.]

368. *Small children wont let you sleep, bigger children wont let you live.*

[The proverb of Parents with a mixed age-range of trying offspring.]

369. *Shallow streams make the most din.*

[It is the same with people whether from England or not.]

370. *Stretch your arm no further than your arm will reach.*

[This is usually no great challenge for those born and bred in Yorkshire.]

371. *Shrouds have no pockets and therefore surely here is a business opportunity for someone of an enterprising inclination.*

[Shrouds have no pockets.]

372. *Starve the problems and feed the opportunities.*

[The proverb of a Restaurant Owner.]

373. *Skeletons are merely the result of striptease dances that have gone too far.*

[The proverb of a misinformed Rag and Bone Dealer.]

Thomas Crapper 1836-1910

T

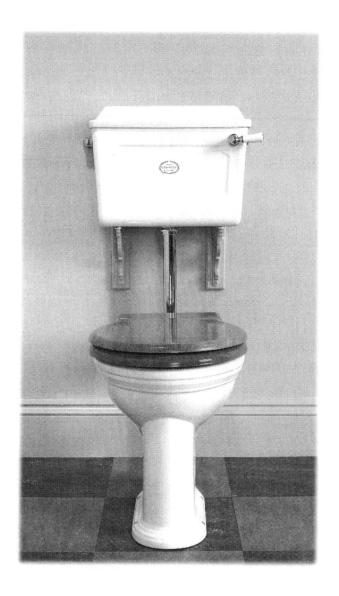

374. *The early bird may get the worm but the second mouse gets the cheese.*

[The proverb of a Mousetrap Salesman.]

375. *The faintest ink is more powerful than the strongest memory.*

[The proverb of a Stationary Supplier.]

376. *The higher you climb up the ladder the more people can see your arse.*

[The proverb of a Window Cleaners Assistant.]

377. *The man who removes a mountain begins by carrying away small stones.*

[The proverb of a Quarry Owner.]

378. *The world is full of willing people; some willing to work and others willing to let them.*

[The proverb of a Job Centre Manager who was also a Sage.]

379. *Take a hair of the dog that bit you and the dog will doubtless bite you again.*

[The proverb of a cautious Englishman whose dog wasn't too pleased having part of its' coat tugged out.]

380. *The most beautiful women are made for lovers who lack imagination.*

[The proverb of a man who either had no imagination or a wife that was less than beautiful.]

381. *To the world you may just be one person but to one person you may be the world.*

[The proverb of a man wearing context lenses.]

382. *Those who play the game do not see it as clearly as those who watch.*

[The proverb of a sharp eyed Rugby League fan commenting on the ability of the referee.]

383. *The best things come in small packages.*

[The proverb of someone who was grateful by nature but who never in his life received a large package.]

384. *Travel may well broaden the mind but at todays' prices it tends to have quite the opposite effect on the wallet.*

[The proverb of a thrifty Armchair Traveller.]

385. *To travel around the world it is necessary to have the mouth of a hog, the legs of a stag, the eyes of a falcon, the ears of an ass, the shoulders of a camel, the face of an ape and, moreover, a forked tongue with which to flatter everyone.*

[The proverb of a man who presumably met some rather strange and perhaps 'beastly' characters whilst journeying far from home.]

386. *The most deadly of wild beasts is a backbiter and, of tame beasts, a flatterer.*

[The proverb of a Zoo Keeper referring to some of the visitors observed at his zoo.]

387. *Trouble brings experience, experience brings wisdom and wisdom is a treasure for all time.*

[A creative statement of defence by an acne-encrusted youth arrested by the local police for being drunk and disorderly in a public place.]

388. *The way to an English mans' heart is through his ribcage.*

[The proverb of a Cardiac Surgeon.]

389. *To the jaundiced eye all things look yellow.*

[Literally doubtful but anecdotally useful.]

390. *The Old believe everything, the Middle Aged suspect everything and the Young know everything.*

[The proverb of a family man.]

391. *There is a skeleton in every cupboard.*

[The proverb of a Museum Curator.]

392. *There is more than one way to skin a cat.*

[The proverb of a Taxidermist.]

393. *Two wrongs may not make a right but three rights certainly make a left.*

[The proverb of a Motorist lost in a large city centre.]

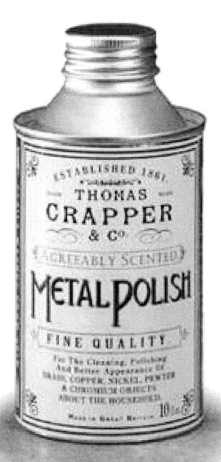

394. *Under the thorns grow the roses.*

[The proverb of a determined Gardener keen to pursue his uncomfortable weeding.]

395. *Unkissed, unkind.*

[The proverb of a rejected and dejected individual who associated lack of tactile stimulation to ruthless and unethical heartlessness.]

396. *Use soft words and hard arguments.*

[The proverb of a Double Glazing Salesman, door to door religious zealot and Wheelie Bin Operative attempting to collect money owed.]

397. *United we stand, divided we fall.*

[The motto of The Rather Terribly Dizzy Club of Great Britain.]

398. *Variety is the spice of life and adventure is the gravy.*

[The proverb of a food fanatic.]

399. *Visit your Aunt but not every day of the year.*

[The proverb of everyones' Aunt.]

W

400. *Walls have ears and this may be attributed to buildings being too close to Nuclear Power Stations.*

    [Walls have ears.]

401. *We all get heavier as we get older because we carry so much more information in our heads than we did when we were younger.*

    [What other reason could there possibly be?!]

402. *When the cat's away the goldfish can rest peacefully.*

    [When the cat's away the mice will play.]

403. *Watch your thoughts for they become words.*
    Watch your words for they become actions.
    Watch your actions for they become habits.
    Watch your habits for they become character.
    Watch your character for it becomes your destiny.

    [The proverb of a seasoned Watcher.]

404. *When you live in the past it costs you the present.*

    [The proverb of a Time-Traveller.]

405. *Work is the curse of the drinking classes.*

    [The proverb of a Pub Landlord.]

406. *What you lose on the swings will often have been stolen by an opportunistic thief.*
    He will rarely leave it anywhere near the roundabouts.

    [What you lose on the swings you will gain on the roundabouts.]

407. *When alone we have our thoughts to watch, in our families, our tempers and in society, our tongues.*

[Another beauty from the seasoned Watcher.]

408. *When the student is ready the Master will appear.*
Then again, when he is not at all ready the Master also often appears.
It happened to me regularly at school and I was often placed in detention as a result.

[M. A. Lee 2004.]

409. *Wherever you may be let your wind go free.*
Whether in church or in chapel, worry not, let it rattle.

[Frank. W. Lee 1926-1988]

410. *Walls are the notebooks of fools.*

[The proverb of the Manager of the local councils' Graffiti Cleaning Department.]

411. *Whoever wants to buy a house must examine the roof and whoever wants to take a wife must look carefully at her Mother.*

[The proverb of an Estate Agent considering marriage and mindful of the ancient adage 'Like Mother, Like Daughter.']

412. *When people only talk about the things they understand a great silence will descend upon the world.*

[Even if this happened everywhere else it would and could never happen in Huddersfield.]

413. *When one is in love a cliff becomes a meadow.*

[The proverb of a besotted and highly dangerous Rock Climber whose last words were "Oops – A daisy".]

414. *When an ass is happy he dances on the ice.*

[The proverb of a Winter Sports Enthusiast.]

415. *When fortune turns against you even jelly breaks your teeth.*

[The proverb of an unlucky gentleman who was reduced to chewing with his gums.]

416. *Words have no wings but they can fly a thousand miles.*

[The proverb of an Airline Pilot.]

417. *Wealth is like a hair in the nose; it hurts to be separated.*

[The proverb of a Banker.]

418. *Worry is like a rocking chair, it keeps you going but gets you absolutely nowhere.*

[The proverb of an anxious Furniture Maker.]

X, Y, Z

419. *You cannot get to the top by sitting on your bottom.*

[Traditional.]

420. *Your future lies before you like a field of driven snow,*
So be careful how you tread it for every step will show.

[The proverb of a Cross-country Skier.]

421. *Youth is the infinite wisdom of inexperience.*

[The proverb of a Cynic with hindsight who was once a youth himself.]

422. *Youth is not an age – it is a state of mind.*

[The proverb of an Eighty Year Old Wishful Thinker.]

423. *Yorkshire born and Yorkshire bred, strong in the arm and good in bed.*

[The uncorrupted version of the proverb 'Yorkshire born and Yorkshire bred, strong in the arm and weak in the head.']

424. *Zeal without Prudence is Frenzy.*

[The proverb of a man whose nickname was Frenzy and called only by his first name, Zeal, by his girlfriend, Prudence. It was so very, very confusing for all involved.]

By the same Author and published by Robson Books

'Written In Jest' ISBN: 1 86105 577 3
[Foreword by Michael Palin]

This book is essentially an amazing and memorable collection of spoof job applications for incredible positions such as Harbour Master for Wigan Pier, Official Government Scapegoat and even Stable Boy for the Four Horses of the Apocalypse and a host of replies from such individuals as Black Rod, The Archbishop of Canterbury and even The Duke of Edinburgh guaranteed to provide hours of laughter and entertainment.

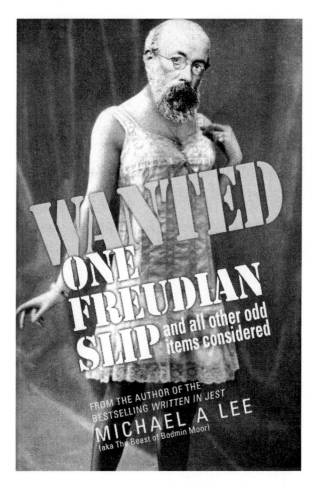

'Wanted: One Freudian Slip' ISBN: 1 86105 680 X

Within the pages of Michael Lee's second book there are letters of a most amusing nature whereby attempts are made to acquire a range of odd items and advice from a miscellany of individuals in high profile positions. Beginning with a request of Next Retail Ltd to supply him with a Freudian slip for his wife's birthday present Lee pursues his quirky quest with more and more outlandish suggestions.

Corporate ladders, spare bubbles for a spirit level and even enquiries around his 'lost umph' to London Underground Lost Property are all par for the course.